Leonardo

Electa/Art Books International

Leonardo

The age in which Leonardo lived was certainly one of the most stimulating and one of the richest in innovatory and creative ferment. After the rebirth of the humanities and the revival of the arts in the period from 1450 to 1550, man, now the "centre of the world," was able to greatly widen the horizons of his knowledge. The invention of the printing press, an invaluable means of diffusing culture, and the discovery of new continents and civilisations were only two aspects of that remarkable period of history in which Leonardo da Vinci lived and worked. His extremely versatile mind ranged over every possible area of science, technology and art, searching in every field for the common mechanisms and fundamental laws which govern and create natural phenomena. Almost nothing is known about the early activity of Leonardo, who was born in 1452 near Vinci, a small town not far from Florence. The Florentine artistic milieu, and in particular the workshop of Andrea Verrocchio, where between about 1469 and 1478 he served his first apprenticeship, were of fundamental importance for his later activity. In Milan, where he lived from 1482 to 1499, inspired by the circle of literati, artists and scientists who gravitated towards the court of Ludovico il Moro, he threw himself with ever-growing passion into the study of mathematics, anatomy, mechanics, optics, hydraulics and botany. The paintings he executed in Milan show the close links that existed between his scientific and artistic research. In the years after he left Milan, which he spent in Florence, Milan again and Rome, Leonardo's interests grew in an eclectic fashion, and he expressed them through inventions, plans, draw-

Self Portrait, detail, ca. 1512. Turin, Biblioteca Reale.

ings and notes on a great variety of topics. Nevertheless, he continued to dedicate himself to painting, which he considered to be the highest form of artistic expression. It is significant that he kept with him during the years he spent in France (1516–1519), until his death, the work which was the high point of his artistic and scientific research, a painting which has always been recognised as one of the great masterpieces of all time, the *Mona Lisa* (Plates 35, 36), which not long ago was defined as "the painted autobiography of the artist."

The Florentine Period (1452–1482)

It is quite surprising to discover that the amount of certain biographical information regarding Leonardo is extremely limited. Despite the enormous quantity of manuscripts and drawings which have remained as a precious inheritance, contemporary accounts are few and far between, there are not many letters and only a handful of drawings and paintings can be dated with certainty. Illegitimate child of a notary called Pietro d'Antonio and a certain Caterina, Leonardo was born near Vinci on 15 April 1452. In 1469 his father moved with the family to Florence. Leonardo, who was then seventeen years old, was admitted to the workshop of Andrea Verrocchio. He remained there for about eight years, at first absorbing the basic achievements of the Florentine Renaissance, learning from his master greater fluency in composition, and then, following his own natural disposition, rebelling against the intellectual rigidity, the linear style and the harshness of form which was typical of much Florentine painting in the second half of the Quattrocento. In 1482 Leonardo left Florence for Milan, placing his skills at the disposal of the Sforza family. It is generally extremely difficult to establish the precise responsibility of Leonardo for the paintings produced by Verrocchio's workshop, given the way the work was organised, which required close collaboration between the pupils. On the other hand, there can be no doubt regarding the drawing of the *Arno Landscape* (Plate 1) in the Uffizi, the first work to be dated by Leonardo, on the basis of an inscription in his hand with the date 5 August 1473.

A year after his enrolment in the painters' guild in the Uffizi drawing the artist displayed a new way of looking at nature. The world was exactly as it appeared to him, with the atmosphere no longer perfectly transparent, but forming a filter between the sight and the image, thus changing visual perception. The drawing already foreshadowed the interest, which he then continued to develop for the rest of his life, in natural phenomena and his concept of art as a means of investigating these. Moreover the first sample of the young Leonardo's painting skills generally recognised by scholars fully confirms this disposition. The child-like face of the angel on the left of Verrocchio's *Baptism of Christ* (Plates 2, 3) is modelled with extremely delicate gradations of colour. The lineaments seem to dissolve due to the light which softens the outlines, but which at the same time gives life to the effects of extremely delicate sfumato in the represention of the complexion and the wonderful lightness of the hair as it cascades in shimmering ripples. The landscape in the background is similarly wrapped in an atmospheric space that seems, through a mixture of form, colour and light, to blend the various

Study for the *Adoration of the Magi*
(facsimile), c. 1481. Florence, Gabinetto
dei disegni e delle stampe degli Uffizi
(original in Paris, Musée du Louvre, Cabinet des dessins).

elements of nature in a cosmic synthesis. Still clearly influenced by the teaching of Andrea Verrocchio is the Uffizi *Annunciation* (Plate 4). The overall composition of the scene — with the angel on the left separated from the Virgin by a lectern, the horizon placed two-thirds of the way up the picture and the villa behind the Madonna — should be attributed to a compositional pattern which was already in use and reveals the influence of a certain academic rigidity. But the extraordinary sequence of tones and luminosity of the image, the meticulous attention given to the elements of the natural world and the stupendously atmospheric quality with which the landscape beyond the low garden wall is depicted, confer on the painting a distinction and charm which is already very definitely typical of Leonardo's manner. The subsequent works increasingly emphasized the progressive formation in the artist's mind of a concept of painting as an ideal expression of his scientific knowledge. The portrait of *Ginevra de' Benci* (Plate 6), painted between 1474 and 1477, has proved to be of great interest. The woman, who was portrayed contrary to the aesthetic canons of Botticelli which were dominant at the time — with their expression of extreme linear sensitivity and a timeless ideal of female beauty — presents strongly individual facial features, artistically created by means of colour and light. In fact, the almost full – face portrayal of the girl allowed the artist to reduce the role of the linear profile to a minimum. The face, with its large flattened volumes, is delicately modelled by extremely subtle gradations of tone, while its pale luminosity is resplendent against the background of a spiky bush which is silhouetted against the sky, allowing us to glimpse, at the sides, a landscape of water and trees. Shortly after this Leonardo executed two paintings, both depicting the Virgin and Child. The *Virgin with the Flowers* (Plate 7) displays stylistic features which were then to become typical of the artist. The light which penetrates from the arched windows in the background and, at the same time, illuminates the image from the front, is diffused over the figures making their stately volumes vibrate and giving the flesh the first extremely delicate effect of sfumato. On the other hand, a warmer chromatic density of light and a more accentuated rounding of the forms are characteristic of the *Benois Madonna* (Plate 8), which was probably painted around 1478. The composition of the painting pivots on the small flower which the Virgin is offering to the Infant Christ. Around it revolves the tender interplay of hands and the exchange of glances of the protagonists, who are completely engrossed in the intimacy of this family scene. The complete stylistic maturity of the artist is emphasized by the way the bodies of the Madonna and Child fit naturally together, by the sfumato of the soft outlines of the figures, which seem to quiver with life and vibrate in the density of the atmosphere, and, above all, by the great sensitivity with which the intimate emotional bonds linking mother and child are depicted.

However, the painting which bears witness to the great progress which the artist had made in his ceaseless inquiry into the basic principles of nature and the deepest secrets of the human soul before his departure for Milan is the *Adoration of the Magi* (Plate 10). Leonardo interpreted the traditional subject in a revolutionary and intensely dra-

Model for the Trivulzio monument, 1506. Budapest, Szépmüvészeti Múzeum.

matic manner, with all his interest focused on the profound religious significance of Christ's birth. The crowd, greatly perturbed by the event, is gathered around the figure of the Virgin and Child, the pivot of the whole composition. The Magi prostrate themselves as they offer their gifts, while the gesticulating crowd is not able to control its feelings and the agitation of its movements seems to be transmitted from one figure to another. In the background the magnificent architectural ruins and the skirmish of warriors on horseback symbolise that part of the world and of humanity not yet aware of the promise of salvation. Not very distant from the unfinished painting of the *Adoration of the Magi* was *Saint Jerome* (Plate 11). The particular posture of the figure gives special emphasis to Leonardo's anatomical interests, which were focused at that time on problems concerning the dynamics of the human body in space. The repentant saint, depicted as he beats his breast, is kneeling down or is about to stand up, as is shown by the bending of the knee, while the sculptural representation of the body fits in very well with the extreme fluidity of the painting's execution.

The Milanese Period (1482–1499)

When Leonardo reached Milan in 1482 he found a particularly lively and stimulating intellectual climate. During the time of Ludovico il Moro the Sforza court became, almost in competition with Florence, a refined centre of the liberal arts, which attracted scientists, artists and men of letters such as Bramante, the mathematician Luca Pacioli and the musician Franchino Gaffurio. During his sixteen – year stay in Milan Leonardo's exceptional versatility in various fields of science, technology and art seem to have been in al-

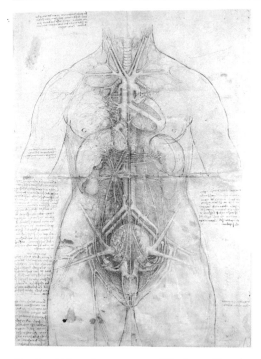

Study of female anatomy. Windsor, Royal Library.

most constant demand by the Sforza court. In fact, he could be seen hard at work around 1489–1490 as the brilliant inventor of elaborate stage machinery and mechanical contrivances for jousts and court pageants, as a designer of costumes for masquerades and tournaments and as a skilled improviser of poetry, fables and riddles. In the same period, as an expert on architecture, he applied himself to studying the problem of the tambour of Milan cathedral and he was consulted, together with Francesco di Giorgio Martini about the completion of Pavia cathedral. In his role as court engineer he tackled the question of schemes involving the management of water in the area, planning locks, canals and irrigation systems. In particular, around 1494, he was concerned with irrigation and drainage works at La Sforzesca, the ducal estate near Vigevano.

But it was above all as a painter that Leonardo revealed a capacity that was so innovative that it upset the traditional canons of Lombard painting of the time. The first example in Milan of this new artistic vision was the painting known as the *Virgin of the Rocks*, central altarpiece of the polyptych executed from 1483 onwards for the altar of a chapel in the church of San Francesco Grande. It was commissioned by the Confraternity of the Immaculate Conception and was painted with the collaboration of the brothers Evangelista and Ambrogio de' Predis (Plates 12, 13; Plates 14–16). First of all, the painting expresses a new vision of nature, which is created anew by the artist by means of a careful analysis of its phenomena. Consequently there is a new way of depicting space, which is no longer conceived according to the principles of perspective, but rather it is created "naturally" by means of the atmosphere, that is to say by the almost imperceptible fusion of air, light and shade that at the same time both envelopes and forms everything. The figures, too, are produced by the natural effect of light and imperceptible gradations of shade on their bodies, which thus acquire the extreme delicacy of their lineaments and the subtle plasticity which are the very basis of Leonardo's sfumato.

The immediate repercussion of this new way of looking at art on the painters of the Lombard school could be noticed in portraiture, a field in which Leonardo introduced a real artistic revolution to Milan. In fact, the *Portrait of a Musician* in the Pinacoteca Ambrosiana (Plate 17), the *Lady with an Ermine* in Cracow (Plates 18, 19) and the portrait of a lady in the Louvre, known as *La Belle Ferronière* (Plates 20, 21), threw the traditional concepts of Milanese portraitists into disarray, accustomed as they were to portraying the sitter with a profile view, in accordance with a taste which was still typically heraldic. While the attribution of the *Portrait of a Musician* in the Pinacoteca Ambrosiana has often been debated in the past, more recent scholarly opinion has generally agreed that it is by the hand of Leonardo, in some cases, however, accepting that there may have been limited assistance by Ambrogio de' Predis in the lower part of the painting. The portrait makes it very clear which direction Leonardo's pictorial research was taking him. The sitter's bust, which seems to revolve in space and intersect the surface of the painting obliquely, and the keen psychological insight of the face, are all expressions of his increasingly profound studies of the dynamics of the body and the representa-

Study of heads, 1478. Florence, Galleria degli Uffizi.

tion of the workings of the human soul. The same elements are arranged with greater compositional skill and a better command of painting techniques in the *Lady with an Ermine*, which may be considered to be one of the highest expressions of Leonardo's art, fruit of the anatomical studies to which the artist had devoted himself for many years. The bust of the girl, a masterpiece of grace and elegance, forms a sinuous spiral in space and concludes splendidly with a face which displays an extraordinary expression of intensity and restrained emotion. The image is infused with life by the shaft of light that practically shapes its structure, illuminating the lady's face, descending her shoulder and falling on her arms which hug the brilliantly white ermine. The climax of Leonardo's activity in Milan is the *Last Supper*, which was painted between 1495 and 1497 in the refectory of the monastery of Santa Maria delle Grazie (Plates 22–24). In fact, it is the conclusion, at their highest point, of his carefully meditated studies of the human spirit.

On hearing Christ firmly announce His imminent betrayal, the Apostles' great excitement seems to abate, and then take artistic form in harmonious unity, through the skilled arrangement of the forms, movements and gestures of the figures, depicted larger – than – life and rhythmically grouped in threes. Also the way the perspective is constructed—thereby extending and amplifying through the use of illusionistic effects the real architectural space of the room—and the brightly – lit landscape that it is possible to see through the windows in the background lend the whole scene unprecedented strength and monumental grandeur.

The Mature Years (1500–1519)

Following the sudden fall of the Sforzas with the invasion of the French troops of Louis XII, Leonardo, who was now famous all over Italy, left Milan together with his friend, Luca Pacioli. It is very likely that he took with him manuscripts covered with notes and observations, together with loose sheets, notebooks and sketchpads crammed with profiles, portraits, caricatures, faces of monstrous or deformed beings and anatomical details which were astonishing for the beauty and precision of the draughtsmanship. After a brief stay in Vaprio d'Adda, at the home of his favourite pupil, Francesco Melzi, Leonardo went to Mantua, where he was a guest of the Gonzagas for a brief period. In an attempt to prevent him from leaving, Isabella d'Este commissioned her portrait, the cartoon for which, is now in the Louvre (Plate 25). In March 1500 Leonardo stayed in Venice in order to offer his services as a military engineer, then in August of that year he returned to Florence, where he was a guest in the monastery of the Serviti alla Santissima Annunziata. He stayed there until 1506. In this period the artist executed paintings which constituted the basis for the evolution of the entire art of the Cinquecento. A composition with Saint Anne, the Virgin and Child and the infant Saint John seemed to capture Leonardo's attention at that time. In fact, this is simply a further development of a theme—that of the pyramidal structure—which had been tackled previously in the *Virgin of the Rocks*. The importance which this theme had acquired in his creative activity is evidenced by the cartoon in the National Gallery in London (Plate 27) and the painting in the Louvre (Plates 29, 30),

Folio of studies from the Codex Atlanticus, 1483-1518. Milan, Biblioteca Ambrosiana.

which probably date from the beginning of the second decade of the sixteenth century, as well as a large number of sketches and preliminary drawings. The London cartoon displays a wonderful balance between art and nature and between matter and spirit. The masterly construction of the group and the compactness and the monumental grandeur of the forms match the naturalness of the movements of the figures, the delicate flow of the drapery, the expressive intensity of the faces and the infinite gentleness of the glances. Mary, Saint Anne, the Child and the infant Saint John are the complete expression of the poetry of the "spirit and breath" which was so characteristic of the Apostles in the *Last Supper*, but with a more restrained

and profound emotional content, and displaying faultlessness of form which became a manifestation of the harmonious perfection of creation. The painting constitutes the conclusive point of the research. The solidity and compactness of the London group is broken up in the Paris painting by more accentuated dynamics of the forms. The "vibrations" which seem to emanate from the rocks in the foreground and the masterly organisation of the movements of the figures—they spontaneously intertwine, embrace each other and then separate in accordance with a harmonious flow of rhythms that have been carefully calculated but seem to be natural—are then subjected by the artist to rational vision. The variety of the phenomena

Study for the head of the apostle James in the *Last Supper* and architectural sketches, c. 1495. Windsor, Royal Library.

Study for the *Last Supper* and architectural sketches, c. 1495. Windsor, Royal Library.

of reality is thus expressed through a geometrical composition which reflects the absolute harmony of the universe, nature and art. In 1502 Leonardo spent a brief period as architect and military engineer in the employ of Cesare Borgia. On his return to Florence in March 1503, the artist was commissioned by the gonfalonier (chief magistrate) of the Republic, Pier Soderini, to paint an enormous fresco celebrating the victory of the Florentines over the Milanese troops of Filippo Maria Visconti in the famous battle of Anghiari in 1440 on one of the walls of the new Sala del Gran Consiglio in Palazzo Vecchio. Neither drawings of the whole painting nor details of the subsidiary motives of Leonardo's majestic work have survived. It is only through a number of engravings and a few copies that the central motive of the composition is known to us. This was the furious struggle of horses and horsemen for the conquest of the standard, the symbol of the city.

In 1506 Leonardo once again left Florence for Milan, where he had been invited by the French governor, Charles d'Amboise. Besides the *Battle of Anghiari* (Plates 31, 32), while he was in Florence he had begun—according to Vasari—the portrait of *Mona Lisa* (Plates 35, 36) and the painting, which was later lost, of *Leda with the Swan* (Plate 26). These were evidence, together with a number of drawings depicting *Neptune with the Seahorses*, of the artist's interest in mythological themes, in particular those which could become the embodiment of the power of nature. In Milan he stayed until 1513. Here he engaged in architectural and hydraulic engineering work, he devoted himself to the study of the equestrian statue for Gian Giacomo Tri-

Armored Vehicles with Scythes, ca. 1485. Turin, Biblioteca Reale.

vulzio (1511–1512), executed the painting of the *Virgin and Saint Anne* (Plates 29, 30) now in the Louvre and, lastly, with assistants, completed the second version of the *Virgin of the Rocks* (Plates 14–16). In this period Leonardo was increasingly absorbed by mathematical and scientific studies; he investigated these interests more thoroughly in Rome, where he moved in 1513. In this city he was accommodated in the Vatican in the Villa del Belvedere with the patronage of Giuliano de' Medici. The artist, who by this time was getting on in years, was averse to the ostentation of the Roman art milieu, which was dominated by Raphael and his circle. Generally leading an isolated life, he executed, among other things, an extraordinary series of drawings on the theme of the *Deluge* (Plate 37), which clearly reveal the unease of the later years of the great artist's life and the crisis of his notion of man as the centre of the universe and mirror of its harmonious perfection. During the years he was in Milan and Rome, Leonardo returned to the theme of the human figure, completing two works of maximum interest—the so – called *Bacchus* (Plate 33) and *Saint John the Baptist* (Plate 34)—which embody a new ideal of beauty which was ambiguous and indeterminate and which was wholly realized in the *Mona Lisa* (Plates 35, 36). This painting, together with *Saint John the Baptist* and the *Virgin and Saint Anne*, was taken by the artist to France in 1517. Loaded with honours, designated by Francis I "premier peintre, architecte et méchanicien du roi," Leonardo resided in the château of Cloux, near Amboise, until his death on 2 May 1519, dedicating himself to his research and to his perturbing drawings on the theme of the *Deluge*. Leonardo spent a great deal of time on the portrait of a lady, which he began sometime between 1503 and 1506 and which was to become the most famous of all his paintings, working on it until his final years, in a ceaseless quest for formal perfection. The painting embodied all Leonardo's experience and was the sublime synthesis of his studies of natural phenomena and of the movements of the human body that the artist had tackled, investigated in depth and attempted to give tangible form to for all his life. The woman in the portrait does not embody an ideal of female beauty, but she becomes the crystallisation of the human individual who sums up in herself, with perfect balance, all the possible states of nature. It is through the medium of painting, taken to a level of extreme technical refinement, that we are able to comprehend the profundity of Leonardo's thought. The passages of tone, colour and luminosity, which are ever subtler and more delicate, the sfumato which is ever softer and more enveloping and layers of glazes which are ever lighter and more transparent, confer on the forms of the woman's body, as well as on the mountains and the expanses of water in the landscape, that margin of indeterminacy which is the expression of perpetual transformation and the eternal renewal of life and nature.

The Legacy

Leonardo da Vinci's legacy is enormous. The exceptional nature of his talent, the multiplicity of his practical skills and the power of his intellect were already universally recognised during his lifetime, while his fame and prestige have never ceased to grow over the centuries. However, it is only relatively recently—more or less from the beginning of the century—that besides Leonardo the artist, at first timorously and then, in time, more clearly, thanks to continuous scholarly inquiry, an unknown Leonardo has begun to take shape. The unfamiliar figure who has been rediscovered made important contributions to mathematics, optics, physics and science in general. The influence of his painting on the art of the Cinquecento is inestimable. Paintings such as the *Virgin of the Rocks* or the *Last Supper*, portraits like the *Musician* and the *Lady with an Ermine* were a constant point of reference for the later generations of Lombard painters, who immediately assimilated Leonardo's iconographic and stylistic innovations, albeit with results that were sometimes decidedly mediocre. Obviously the effects of Leonardo's art were not limited just to Lombardy, but had far-reaching repercussions all over Europe in the sixteenth century. Thus Giorgione, Dürer, Raphael, Michelangelo and Correggio could not help but continuously refer to Leonardo's masterpieces and compare their own work with his. Leonardo has always enjoyed undisputed critical and literary acclaim. But the mythical nineteenth-century image of the great—but admittedly somewhat eccentric—artistic genius for a long time prevented a more objective study of his personality. Only in the last few decades has the study, transcription and interpretation of the great quantity of drawings and annotations entrusted to the surviving codices thrown new light on the romantic picture of the artist. In its place there is another, still greater image of Leonardo, which is slowly taking shape on a historical and philological basis.

1

1. Arno Landscape, *1473,*
pen and brown ink and wash
on paper, 19.6 × 28 cm.
Gabinetto dei disegni e delle
stampe degli Uffizi, Florence.
The inscription in the artist's
hand in the margin of the
sheet allows us to date this
drawing 5 August 1473, so
that it is considered to be the

oldest dated work by Leonardo.
The work is extraordinarily
innovatory for the period,
above all because it depicts
a real location rather than an
unspecified landscape, and
also because of the particular
way the artist represents
nature.
This is observed with

unprecedented perceptiveness
and recreated on paper by
means of dynamic pen strokes
which immediately depict the
world as it really is, no longer
forming outlines, but creating
a closely-woven network of
vibrating lines, which build up
a spatial dimension composed
of atmosphere, air and light.

2

2, 3. Andrea Verrocchio and Leonardo da Vinci, Baptism of Christ, *c. 1472–1475, panel, 177 × 151 cm. Galleria degli Uffizi, Florence. This painting was executed by Verrocchio for the church of San Salvi in Florence. According to the oldest sources, the face of the angel on the left, with its blurred outlines and delicate sfumato, was by the hand of the pupil. However, more recently it has been thought that Leonardo was also responsible for the left part of the landscape in the background, a steep-sided valley along which flows a river that in the foreground reflects the light shining from above. Scholars have come to this conclusion as a result of a stylistic examination and X-ray analysis which have ascertained that the angel's face and Christ's hair, as well as some parts of the landscape in the background, were completed in oils over a ground prepared with tempera.*

4

4. Annunciation, c. 1474, panel, 104 × 217 cm. Galleria degli Uffizi, Florence.
Coming from the church of San Bartolomeo di Monteoliveto, the panel was for a long time thought to be by Domenico Ghirlandaio. The attribution to the young Leonardo dates back to the second half of the last century and caused perplexity on the part of many scholars. But in the light of the most recent studies of the different stages of Leonardo's activity as a painter, it seems to have been fully confirmed. The archangel, kneeling on a carpet of meticulously painted flowers, is perhaps the most successful part of the painting; the drapery which he is wearing, especially the sleeve, displays a marvellous eye for colour and composition. In the distance, beyond a row of trees with their varied silhouettes, can be seen, wrapped in the clear dawn light, a landscape with a small town overlooking a bay dotted with ships.

5

5. Study for the Sleeve
of the Angel in the
Annunciation, *c. 1474,
red chalk, 8.5 × 9.5 cm.
Christ Church, Oxford.*

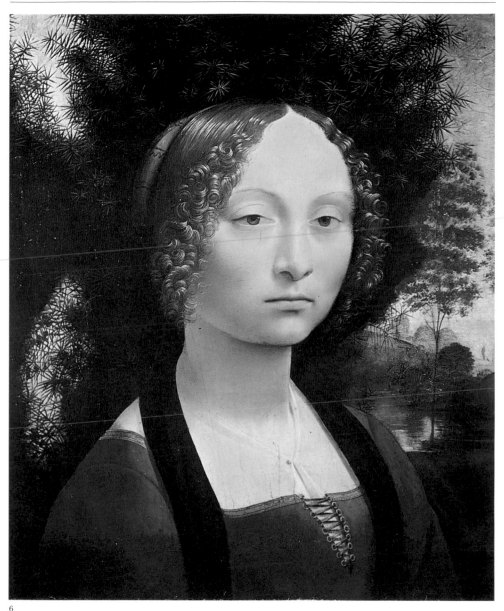

6

6. Ginevra de' Benci, *c. 1474, panel, 42 × 37 cm. National Gallery of Art, Washington. The panel, which is painted on both sides, depicts on the front, according to sixteenth-century sources, the noblewoman Ginevra de'* Benci, daughter of the Florentine banker Amerigo de' Benci, with whom Leonardo was on friendly terms. The girl's name is alluded to by the sprig of juniper encircled by a palm frond and laurel branch which appears on the reverse *of the panel. Since this wreath is truncated at the base, it can be assumed that about a third of the painting has been cut off. It is possible that the lower part of the painting, in which the hands were represented, was never brought to completion.*

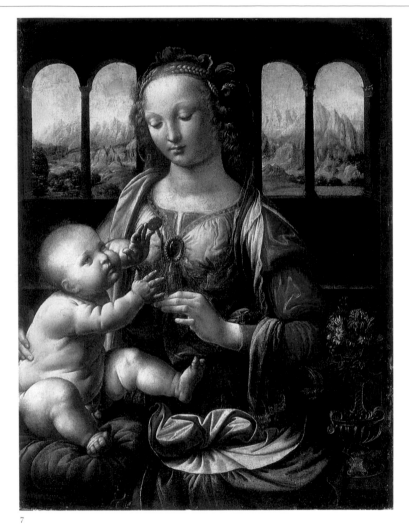

7

7. Virgin with the Flowers, *1475–1478, panel, 62 × 47 cm. Alte Pinakothek, Munich.* *The painting is one of Leonardo's early works; in fact, the links with Verrocchio are still evident. Besides, a number of stylistic features recall the Madonna in the* Annunciation *in the Uffizi (Plate 4).* *The figure of the Virgin and Child rises in the pictorial space with its imposing structure, while their ample forms are stressed by the light*

from the front which illuminates the Virgin's face and shows up the small folds in the edges of her robe. *The complex interplay of composition and colour in the drapery, the precisely-painted details of the Virgin's plaited hair and a number of stylistic refinements lend a stately, even sumptuous, tone to the scene.*

8. Benois Madonna, *c. 1478, panel, 48 × 31 cm. Hermitage, Leningrad.*

Painted shortly after the Virgin with the Flowers *(Plate 7), it is the work which is most probably one of those referred to in the inscription by Leonardo on a drawing in the Uffizi, according to which in 1478 he began to paint "the two pictures of the Virgin Mary. "Previously attributed to Verrocchio and Lorenzo di Credi, the painting has a number of minor lacunas and has been repainted as a result of past restoration.*

9

9. Study for the Adoration
of the Magi, *c. 1481, pen
and ink, wash and white
heightening, 16.3 × 29 cm.
Gabinetto dei disegni e delle
stampe degli Uffizi, Florence.
This is one of the many studies
and preparatory drawings*

*which Leonardo executed for
the* Adoration of the Magi
*(Plate 10).
Unlike the final composition
this work is still an attempt to
define, in terms of geometry
and perspective, the space
intended to contain the*

*figures. The magnificent
architectural motive was then
surpassed by the Uffizi picture.
Here "atmospheric" space was
dominant, created by the
density of the air, by the effects
of light and by the very
movement of the figures.*

10

10. Adoration of the Magi, 1481–1482, "giallolino" and bistre on panel, 246 × 243 cm. Galleria degli Uffizi, Florence.
In 1481 the monks of San Donato a Scopeto, near Florence, commissioned Leonardo to paint an altarpiece representing the Adoration of the Magi. In fact, this was the only well-documented commission of Leonardo's early Florentine period and the first one in which the artist was engaged on a great work of art. The work is unfinished, with only the underdrawing visible; despite this, besides the simple drawing in green earth, the images are also given life by the application of chiaroscuro with subtle tonal gradations. Leonardo never delivered the work to the monks at Scopeto; in 1496 they replaced it with a painting by Filippino Lippi of the same subject. At present the splendid composition is marred by the presence of a large number of flaws which ought to be removed through cleaning and conservation.

11

11. Saint Jerome, 1481–1482, panel, 103 × 75 cm. Pinacoteca Vaticana, Rome. Despite the lack of documentary evidence or preliminary drawings which allow this work to be associated with Leonardo, there have never been doubts concerning its attribution, and this is fully confirmed by analysis of both technique and style. The recent restoration of the painting, which never got beyond the monochrome stage, has ascertained the existence of traces of past repainting.

12

12, 13. Virgin of the Rocks (Madonna with Child, the Infant Saint John and an Angel), *c. 1483–1490, panel transferred to canvas, 198 × 122 cm. Louvre, Paris. The composition, which was transferred to canvas at the end of the eighteenth century, introduced new iconographic and stylistic concepts to Milan that were to bring about profound changes in the Lombard painting of the period. Leonardo substituted an involved composition, centring on a precise iconographic and symbolic relationship, for the traditional image of the Madonna on a throne holding the Child in her arms. The figures, which form a pyramidal structure, are set in a rocky landscape at the entrance to a cave—the symbol of the mystery and obscurity of nature—in which the almost palpable atmosphere of humid luminosity can be felt to thicken.*

14

14-16. Virgin of the Rocks (Madonna with Child, the Infant Saint John and an Angel), *c. 1495–1508, panel, 189.5 × 120 cm. National Gallery, London.*
The painting, which was painted with the collaboration of his pupil Giovanni Ambrogio de' Predis, was probably executed to substitute *the original work, which was perhaps never delivered to the Confraternity.*
The London painting presents an intentional simplification of the involved iconographic and symbolic contents of the Paris version, while, stylistically, the figures are endowed with greater solidity and are more imposing, their *lineaments accentuated by greater use of chiaroscuro and the cooler tones of his palette. The greater intensity of the shadows, together with a somewhat less meticulous attention to detail, also characterise the immediate surroundings and the distant landscape in the background.*

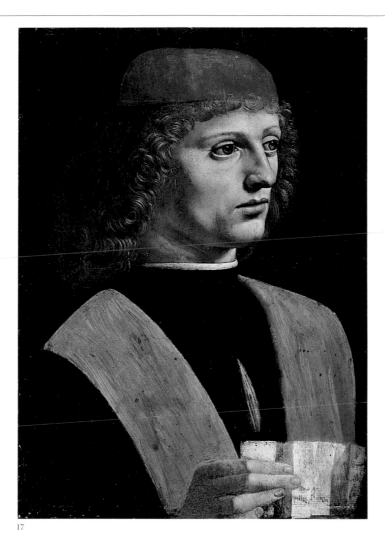

17

17. Portrait of a Musician, 1485–1490, panel, 44 × 32 cm. Pinacoteca Ambrosiana, Milan.
The painting, which is the only male portrait on a panel which can be attributed to Leonardo, dates from the early years of the artist's stay in Milan. While the hair and the face, with their warm tonality of colour, are painted in very great detail and display an extraordinary degree of skill, the robe, the stole and the hand with the scroll definitely seem to be unfinished. The removal, at the beginning of this century, of repainting from the lower part of the painting led to the discovery of the right hand holding a scroll on which there are staves, musical notes and a number of faded letters. The attempts to identify the sitter have, therefore, focused on the most prominent musicians of the Milanese court, in particular Franchino Gaffurio and the Flemish composer Josquin des Pres, but it has not been possible to come to a definite conclusion.

18

18, 19. Lady with an Ermine (Portrait of Cecilia Gallerani?), *c. 1490, panel, 54 × 40 cm. Czartoryski Muzeum, Cracow.*
The young woman has been almost unanimously identified by scholars as Cecilia Gallerani, Ludovico il Moro's cultured and refined mistress. There is a reference to her surname in the Greek name for ermine, which was a symbol of purity and chastity. Despite the fact that some parts are unfinished and others are repainted, this portrait must certainly be considered as one of the artist's finest paintings. The great skill with which Leonardo resolved the problem of the dynamics of the human body in space, the intense psychological introspection of the face, the vivacious expression of the eyes, together with an elegantly refined appearance, make this painting one of the great masterpieces, not only of Leonardo's oeuvre, but also of Renaissance portraiture in general.

20

20, 21. La Belle Ferronière, *c. 1495–1499, panel, 62 × 44 cm. Louvre, Paris. There has been considerable controversy regarding the attribution to Leonardo of the portrait of a lady known as "La Belle Ferronière." Now, with only a few exceptions, scholars tend to ascribe this painting to the artist because of the evident similarities of style and subject-matter—the dark background, the diagonal positioning of the bust, the body which seems to revolve in space, the intense expression of the eyes—that it has in common with the other two portraits which he executed during his first stay in Milan. The numerous attempts to identify the sitter have not so far been able to produce adequate documentary evidence or find confirmation of an iconographic nature. The hypothesis which has gained the greatest credit among scholarly opinion is that the woman is none other than Cecilia Gallerani who was portrayed by Leonardo, only a few years previously, in the painting now in Cracow (Plates 18, 19).*

22

22–24. Last Supper, *1495–*
1497, tempera and oil on two
layers of intonaco,
460 × 880 cm. Refectory,
Santa Maria delle Grazie,
Milan. Leonardo interpreted
the subject in a wholly
innovatory manner, depicting
the moment of greatest
dramatic tension in the
narration of the Gospels: the
announcement of His
imminent betrayal by Christ,
who is isolated at the centre of
the scene, and the agitated
reaction of the Apostles who
question each other
incredulously, displaying
consternation and
astonishment. The brilliant

way the composition was
structured, thanks to the
adoption of an experimental
pictorial technique, should
have constituted, from
Leonardo's point of view, the
stylistic embodiment of his
research into the inner recesses
of the human spirit, thus
representing the very essence of
his artistic tenets. While his
refusal to adopt the fresco
technique allowed the artist to
give finishing touches, make
improvements and "veil" the
figures, in order to confer
"spirit and breath" on them,
the pigments—bound with
tempera or oily substances on
very thin layers of intonaco—

proved to be extremely
vulnerable to humidity and the
effects of external agents.
Already in the second half of
the sixteenth century a number
of sources refer to the poor
state of conservation of the
painting. Since then, over the
centuries, there have been
numerous attempts at
restoration, some of them
involving additions or
repainting. Plate 22 shows the
work before the most recent
restoration while Plates 23
and 24 are details taken
during restoration.

23

24

25

25. Portrait of Isabella d'Este, *c. 1500, black chalk and pastel on paper, 63 × 46 cm. Louvre, Paris.*
The drawing, which was executed on paper in black and red chalk, is at present in a poor state of conservation. The flesh, especially around the lineaments of the face, is delicately modelled with shades of pink which, with slightly *darker tones, are also to be found in the hair. The folds, the voile and the ribbons which are part of the woman's dress are, on the other hand, faintly drawn with touches of yellow. Along the lines which give shape to Isabella's magnificent dress and define the right hand are still visible the minute pinpricks which were intended to allow very fine* *charcoal powder to filter through to the surface of the painting so that it could reproduce the outline. Despite insistent requests, Leonardo never completed the portrait of the Mantuan noblewoman, just limiting himself to lightly going over in ink the profile and the outline of the hair.*

26

26. Study for the Head
of Leda, *1506–1507, pen
and ink, 35 × 20 cm.
Civiche Raccolte d'Arte al
Castello Sforzesco, Milan.
Leda, the mythical Greek
heroine was the subject of a
painting to which Leonardo
dedicated himself during his
second stay in Florence. The
drawing emphasizes the extent
of the artist's interest in*
*women's hairstyles, something
he had inherited from
Verrocchio. Here he depicts
Leda's hair with truly
surprising complexity and a
high aesthetic level. All that
remains of the painting are
some invaluable descriptions, a
large number of copies and a
few sketches by the artist. These
allow us, however, not only to
follow the stylistic evolution of*
*the theme in Leonardo's
mind—from the kneeling
version to the standing one—
but also to recognise in the
original picture the first
example of a type of drawing,
the so-called "serpentine
figure," which was extremely
popular in the sixteenth
century.*

28

27. The Virgin and Child with Saint Anne, *1499–1508?, light ochre, charcoal, tempera and white heightening, 159 × 101 cm. National Gallery, London. This cartoon in the National Gallery and the one depicting the* Portrait of Isabella d'Este *(Plate 25) are the only cartoons which survive out of the large number which* Leonardo prepared for his paintings. Scholars, in fact, tend to to place the work in the period from 1499, the last year of Leonardo's stay in Milan, to around 1508, the year in which, after his stay in Florence, he returned to the Lombard city. Thanks to the harmonious composition of the forms and the restrained *lyricism of its emotional content, this picture must be considered one of the most sublime expressions of Leonardo's art.*

28. Study for the Virgin and Child with Saint Anne, *c. 1510–1513, pen and ink and charcoal on paper, 12.5 × 10 cm. Gallerie dell'Accademia, Venice.*

29

29, 30. The Virgin and
Child with Saint Anne,
c. 1510–1513, panel,
168 × 122 cm. Louvre,
Paris.
Although this painting—which
was probably executed during
Leonardo's second stay in
Milan—is unfinished and
partly repainted, it is the final
version of the theme which he
had already dealt with in a
previous cartoon, since lost,
and in the composition now
in the National Gallery
in London. The pyramidal
construction of the group is
perfectly balanced, with Saint
Anne at the apex, glancing
towards the Virgin. She, in her
turn, leans down and stretches
out her arms towards her son
who, embracing a lamb,
repeats his mother's
affectionate gesture. It is,
therefore, through the
contemplative intimacy of this
family scene, pervaded
by a wonderful atmosphere
of peacefulness, that the theme
of the Incarnation of Christ is
expressed in allegorical form.
Behind the group, there is a
fantastic vista of mountain
peaks, glaciers and watery
wastes, wrapped in icy mists
and frozen in an atmosphere
of impenetrable silence where
time has ceased to exist.

31

31. Study for the Battle
of Anghiari, Skirmishes
between Horsemen and
Foot Soldiers, *1504, pen and
ink on paper, 16.5 × 15.3
cm. Gallerie dell'Accademia,
Venice.*

32

32. Head of a Warrior, c. 1504, chalk, 19.2 × 18.8 cm. Szépmüvészeti Múzeum, Budapest.
This famous head of a warrior, which was drawn on the verso of a sheet in the national museum in Budapest, is one of the very few drawings by Leonardo which almost certainly refer to the battle of Anghiari. The recto of the sheet depicts, instead, the profile of another head of a warrior, which, however, does not display the expressive intensity of the first drawing. Through the dramatic incisiveness of the warrior and the attention given to the details of the face, this analytical study already gives a clear idea of the violent twisting of the bodies and the extreme tension of the composition present in the whole work.

33

33. Bacchus, *1511–1513, canvas, 177 × 115 cm. Louvre, Paris. Originally the painting represented Saint John the Baptist in the desert, but in the second half of the seventeenth century it was transformed into the god Bacchus. Because this radically altered its nature, the painting can neither be* considered to form part of the artist's oeuvre nor to be a significant example of the new aesthetic concept which Leonardo had developed in that period.

34. Saint John the Baptist, *1513–1516, panel, 69 × 57 cm. Louvre, Paris. The painting was probably* executed during the last years of Leonardo's stay in Rome. The figure who is depicted, wrapped in a soft all-embracing shadow, displays that expression of languid ambiguity which was so typical of the artist's last portraits. Here the use of sfumato is excessive, giving the whole image a somewhat ungainly appearance.

36

35, 36. Mona Lisa, *1503–1506/1513, panel, 77 × 53 cm. Louvre, Paris.*
Since Giorgio Vasari's story that the woman portrayed by Leonardo was Mona Lisa, wife of the Florentine merchant Francesco del Giocondo, has proved to be unreliable, the identity of the "Lady on the Balcony" is still a topic of scholarly dispute. The problem is, however, of minor importance compared with the great artistic merits of the painting, which is an unprecedented work in the field of portraiture thanks to the naturalness of the figure's pose, the extreme softness of the drapery, the barely perceptible translucency of the veils which cover her figure and the complexity of the psychological nuances which animate the indefinable expression of her face. The extraordinary tonal and stylistic unity of the painting, the sense of being in a "timeless" dimension which both figure and landscape emanate, are also due to the effect of the layers of paint, which as well as having a vital protective function, tone down and render more uniform the luminosity, intensity and transparency of Leonardo's original colours.

37

37. Deluge, *c. 1516, black chalk, pen and ink on paper, 16.2 × 20.3 cm. Royal Library, Windsor Castle. This work, which was executed in black chalk with touches of yellowish ink, forms part of a series of sixteen drawings dealing with the theme of the Deluge. This terrible apocalyptic vision, dating from the last years of the artist's life, in which all the forces of nature are unleashed with appallingly destructive violence in a catastrophe which obliterates the presence of man, became a concrete expression of Leonardo's extremely dramatic meditation on the universe and all the constituent parts of creation.*

Where to See Leonardo

A tireless and multi-sided genius whose outpouring of work never ceased, Leonardo turned into a slow and painstaking perfectionist when it came to translating this vast sea of studies and notes into concrete form. The net result is embarrassing: the paintings on board are very few, the ambitious equestrian monument to Francesco Sforza was never completed, and not one of the scientific treatises he planned ever saw the light of day. Precisely because of their rarity, Leonardo's works are regarded as milestones of civilisation, and have come to be scattered over a variety of countries. The fundamental points on this itinerary are the places where the master spent most of his life (Florence, Milan, and France), but there are several important deviations from this route.

Works in Italy

It should be pointed out that by Leonardo's "works" we do not just mean his paintings, even though these constitute the salient part of the artist's output: we wish to include here his drawings, architectural projects, and scientific, technical and engineering studies. And even to mention, though only in passing, Leonardo's more "ephemeral" activities, for the festivals of the Sforza family: the staging of the *Festival of the Zodiac* in the Castle in Milan has become proverbial.

Florence

Nothing is left of the fresco of the *Battle of Anghiari* in Palazzo Vecchio: recent tests carried out on the walls, in an attempt to find any remaining fragments, have produced totally negative results. Consequently, all Leonardo's works are concentrated in the Uffizi. There are three paintings, all from his juvenile period, predating his departure for Milan.

The earliest is the *Baptism of Christ*, a solemn composition conceived by Andrea Verrocchio and executed in collaboration with Leonardo at the very beginning of his career. Leonardo was responsible for the angel depicted in profile and the delicate landscape.

This is followed by the *Annunciation*, precious for its details and already showing a keen interest in the psychology of the personages. Finally, the extremely important *Adoration of the Magi*, a large panel that was left unfinished: in contrast to the essentially stationary character of Florentine painting around 1480, Leonardo was seeking a vibrant dynamism, which is revealed in the gestures and expressions.

The Drawing and Print Room of the Uffizi contains some highly important juvenile drawings by Leonardo, including the *Landscape* of 1473, considered the oldest to have come down to us.

Vinci

The commune of Vinci has decided to honour its illustrious son with two initiatives: one is the conservation of the house in which the artist was born, while the other is the setting up, in the local castle, of a museum devoted to Leonardo's inventions and "machines." Drawings and plans have been used to build wooden models of the devices invented by Leonardo.

Milan

Milan is the city where Leonardo spent the longest time. The traces left by the master are numerous, although very often indirect. The Lombard school of painting of the early sixteenth century was strongly influenced by "Leonardism," while the consequences of his advice can be detected in many imposing works of architecture.

Yet the starting point cannot be other than the *Last Supper* painted in the refectory of Santa Maria delle Grazie. Leonardo revolutionized the iconography of this subject, by choosing to represent the moment when Christ announces his betrayal. Unfortunately, the experimental technique that was used to fix the colours has proved extremely ineffective: the recent restoration (still under way) can only confirm the precarious state of this masterpiece. Many copies, varying in size, date, and quality, are to be found in Milan's museums and in churches in Lombardy. For some years now the hypothesis has been put forward that Leonardo also designed the decoration of the ceiling of the Old Sacristy in the same Dominican monastery of Santa Maria delle Grazie.

The Sale delle Asse, the spectacular room in the Castello Sforzesco that Leonardo transformed into a vast pergola, has been almost completely repainted (with the exception of some portions of the lower part of the walls). Important records of Leonardo's presence (drawings and engravings) are to be found in the Raccolta Vinciana, also located in the castle.

The only painting on board by Leonardo in Milan is the penetrating *Portrait of a Musician* in the Pinacoteca Ambrosiana, which also has paintings by followers of Leonardo.

The library of the same institution contains an extremely important collection of manuscripts (the Codex Atlanticus) and drawings by the master.

The Pinacoteca di Brera, although full of paintings by the da Vinci school, contains no work by the master himself: there is a coloured drawing of the *Head of the Redeemer* that is partially attributed to Leonardo and considered a study for or derivation of Christ's face in the *Last Supper*.

The Galleria di Leonardo, the most important section of the Museo della Scienza e Tecnologia, is devoted to his activity as an engineer and inventor. It houses reconstructions of instruments and machines designed by the master, as well as models of his architectural studies. Leonardo also made available his expertise as a hydraulic engineer for imposing schemes for the layout of watercourses (the canals that connect Milan to the river system of Lombardy) and as a mathematician specializing in complex structures for ambitious works of architecture built at the behest of the Sforza family, such as Milan Cathedral, the Piazza Ducale in Vigevano, and Pavia Cathedral.

Other Locations in Italy

The only painting by Leonardo in Italy outside Florence and Milan is the incomplete *Saint Jerome* in the Vatican Art Gallery in Rome.

The drawings that are preserved in other cities, however, are of notable importance. The so-called *La Scapigliata* (Disheveled Woman) in the Galleria Nazionale of Parma can be considered halfway between a drawing and a painting. The Gallerie dell'Accademia in *Venice* contain a highly celebrated group of folios, including the *Proportions of the Human Body*, with the figure of a man set inside a square and a circle; among the other works are the first sketches for the *Last Supper* and studies of *Grotesque Heads* and *Caricatures*. There is another important series in the Biblioteca Nazionale of *Turin*: it includes the famous *Self Portrait* in sanguine.

Works Located Abroad

All of Leonardo's paintings are in private collections and only a very few drawings belong to private individuals.

Great Britain

The royal collection in Windsor Castle, which contains by far the most important set of Leonardo's drawings in the world, may be considered halfway between public and private in status.

Fortunately the fire that ravaged the castle in December 1992 left the works of art in the British royal collection untouched, and in particular came nowhere near the exceptional series of Leonardo's drawings and handwritten notes. Among the most precious of these folios are the large studies for the heads of the apostles in the *Last Supper*; also memorable are the *Studies of Nature*, notes on hydrodynamics, and sketches for the equestrian monuments planned in Milan.

In *London*, more drawings by Leonardo can be found in the British Museum. But the main point of reference is the National Gallery, which has assigned the painter a role of great significance: in fact the marvelous *Cartoon for the Virgin with Saint Anne* has been set at the conclusion of the route taken by organised visits to the new wing of the museum. Alongside it is placed the second version of the *Virgin of the Rocks*, painted by Leonardo's pupils under their master's direct supervision.

France

The Musée du Louvre in *Paris*, with the works dating from the years that Leonardo spent in Amboise and the paintings that have been accumulated over the following centuries, contains about a third of the artist's entire output of paintings, with pictures from every phase of his career.

The sequence opens with the small, juvenile *Annunciation*, originally the predella to an altarpiece painted by his friend Lorenzo di Credi. It is followed by the prestigious first version of the *Virgin of the Rocks* (begun in 1483), the first picture he painted in Milan. He took the effects used to depict nature and atmosphere in the *Virgin of the Rocks* to extraordinary lengths in the *Mona Lisa*, set against a background of typically Pre-Alpine scenery. The portrait is probably the most famous picture in the world and has been reproduced in endless versions, some of them distinctly irreverent.

As a result it has become difficult to appreciate the extraordinary beauty and innovative character of the work, based as it is on subtle interplays of light and psychology.

A further development in the study of the complexity of aspects of nature is to be found in the wonderful *Virgin with Saint Anne*. And in the mysterious image of *Saint John the Baptist*, Leonardo's last work, we find another of his ambiguous smiles.

The Louvre's collection of graphic art also contains some of Leonardo's finest drawings, including anatomical studies and the *Portrait of Isabella d'Este*. Among the other collections of Leonardo's drawings in French museums is the one in the Musée Bonnat in Bayonne, which includes the crude image of the *Hanged Man*.

Other Locations in Europe

The gentle *Madonna del Garofano* from his juvenile period is in the Alte Pinakothek in *Munich*.

A number of significant drawings by Leonardo are located in museums in Eastern Europe. The Hermitage in *Saint Petersburg* houses two panels representing the Madonna and Child: the smiling *Benois Madonna* and the tender *Litta Madonna*.

The gem of the Czartoryski Muzeum is the fascinating and slender *Lady with an Ermine*, a portrait of Ludovico il Moro's lover Cecilia Gallerani.

In addition to a fair number of drawings (including *Studies for the Battle of Anghiari*), the Museum in Budapest possesses a bronze *Knight on a Rearing Horse*, considered by some critics to be the only work of sculpture attributable to Leonardo.

United States

The *Portrait of Ginevra de' Benci* is in the collections of the National Gallery of Art in Washington: the juniper bush in the background of the painting is an allusion to the girl's name.

Anthology of Comments

The painter, or rather draughtsman, has to be solitary, above all when he is busy with speculations and reflections, which, as they continuously appear before his eyes, provide arguments for the memory which should be carefully retained... The eye, in which the splendour of the universe is reflected by the observer, is so excellent that anyone who permits it to be lost, deprives himself of the sight of all the works of nature, in order to see which the soul is content to abide in the prison of the human body, through whose eyes the soul perceives all the various wonders of Nature. (Leonardo da Vinci, *Trattato della Pittura, Codex Vaticano Latino 1270*, c. 1550, Biblioteca Vaticana, Rome)

If the painter wishes to see things of beauty that will enchant him, he may create them. If he wants to see monstrous things that frighten people, or that are clownish and ridiculous, or are truly pitiful then he is free to do it. And if he wishes to create places and wildernesses and cool shady nooks in hot weather, he will paint them, and so will he depict hot places in cold weather. If he desires valleys, if he wishes to cast his eyes over great expanses of countryside from high mountain peaks and if he then wants to observe the horizon of the sea, it is within his power to do so. And the same is true if from low valleys he wishes to see high mountains or from the high mountains he wishes to see low valleys and beaches. And, in effect, that which is in the universe because it is

of the essence or because it is present or is an invention, he has first of all in his mind and then in his hands. And these are so excellent that with the same speed they create proportioned harmony at a single glance, just as the natural world does. (Leonardo da Vinci, *Trattato della pittura, Codex Vaticano Latino 1270*, c. 1550, Biblioteca Vaticana, Rome)

There were in Milan at the time of Viscount Ludovico Sforza, Duke of Milan, some gentlemen in the monastery of the Grazie of the monks of the Dominican order, and in the refectory they stood in silence observing the miraculous and famous last supper of Christ with his disciples which the excellent Florentine painter Leonardo da Vinci was painting at that time, and he was very anxious that whosoever saw his work should freely express his opinion regarding it. He would go there early in the morning and climb up on the scaffolding, because the painting is quite high above the ground. On numerous occasions, and I have seen this with my own eyes, he would not put his brush down from sunrise to dusk, but, forgetting to eat and drink, he would continue to paint. There were then two, three or even four days in which he did not touch his painting, yet he stood sometimes one or two hours a day just looking at it and then he examined it carefully and passed judgements on the figures. I also saw him, when the whim took him, leave at midday, with the sun in the sign of Leo, from the Corte Vecchia where he was making that stupendous clay horse, and come straight to the Grazie, climb onto the scaffolding, take up his brush, give one or two touches to one of the figures and then straightaway leave for another place. (Matteo Bandello, Novella LVIII, in *Novelle*, 1497)

Great gifts are seen to rain down from the celestial spheres on human beings. Often naturally, and sometimes supernaturally, in a single being are excessively concentrated beauty, grace and virtue in such a manner that—whatever this individual may turn his hand to—every action of his is so divine that, leaving all other men behind him, it is manifestly recognised as a thing which only God can bestow and is not acquired by human art. Men saw this quality in Leonardo da Vinci, who, apart from the beauty of his body, which was never lauded sufficiently, displayed infinite grace in everything that he did; and so great was his virtue and such was its nature that, whatever difficult thing he turned his attention to, he was able to conclude with the greatest of ease... Because nature desired to favour him, wherever he turned his thought, mind or spirit, he displayed such excellence in his actions that his perfection of eagerness, vivacity, goodness, handsomeness and charm were never equalled by anyone else. It should be noted that, because of his great ability in art, Leonardo began many things, but did not complete any of them, as it appeared to him that his hand could not add anything to the perfection of art in the things he invented. Moreover he formed in his mind such subtle and wondrous problems that with his hands, however excellent they might have been, he could not have ever created them. And so many were his fantasies that, when philosophising about natural things, he would dedicate himself to studying the properties of grasses and then would go on to observe the motion of the heavens, the phases of the moon and the path of the sun...

It is a wonderful thing that this great master, who, wishing to give maximum relief to the things that he was painting, made such great use of dark shades that he produced dark backgrounds that required blacks that might create gradations of colour and were darker than the other blacks, with the result that the light colours were so much brighter.

Finally he was able to produce a style which was so dark that, as nothing light remained, it seemed to depict a night scene rather than something seen by light of day. But all this was an attempt to give greater relief, to find the true purpose of art and attain perfection... In the art of painting he added to the manner of using oil paints a certain darkness, by means of which modern painters have derived strength and relief for their figures.
(G. Vasari, *Delle Vite de' più eccellenti pittori, scultori et architettori*, 1568, 1906 edition)

Leonardo's character is to be found in his nobility of spirit, in the lucidity of his inventiveness, the breadth of his knowledge, thought and deeds and his wise counsel, which were united to his handsome appearance, justice, reason, wisdom and the separation of right from wrong, the sublimity of light from the baseness of obscurity and ignorance from the boundless glory of truth and charity, the queen of all virtues... In his painting he was dependent on the greatness of his drawing and he achieved this so completely that the figures of men, whether of noble station or humble, were depicted with a great spate of painting, meticulously portraying their characteristics, giving them light and shade as necessary by means of many layers of paint. And in the smaller details, such as the caps, flowing locks and hair in general, flowers, grass, stones and especially the drapery, he so wonderfully and with such skill applied the paint that no mortal eye could desire anything further...

When painting light Leonardo showed that he always wanted to avoid making it too bright, to create a better effect, and he tried to make the dark colours very intense so as to discover their utmost limits. Therefore, with this art he achieved in the faces and the bodies, which he painted marvellously, everything that nature can create. And in this role he was superior to everyone else, to the extent that, in a word, we can describe Leonardo's genius as being divine.
(G.P. Lomazzo, *Idea del Tempio della pittura*, 1590)

Leonardo da Vinci was born before Michelangelo Buonarroti, and he was endowed with a less resolute genius, which was less extensive but more noble... He had two manners of painting: one made use of dark colours which allowed the light colours to stand out marvellously; ...the other was a calmer style and was effected by means of half-tones... In all his styles the grace of his drawing, the expression of his nature and the subtlety of his brushwork triumphed.
(L. Lanzi, *Storia pittorica della Italia*, 1792)

Even though he was a universal genius, Leonardo revealed his greatness above all in his painting. As he was proportioned regularly and perfectly, in comparison with common men he appeared to be an ideal example of humanity. Just as the lucidity and the keenness of the sight refer more appropriately to the intellect, so lucidity and intelligence were peculiar to the artist. He never yielded to the sudden impulses of his matchless original talent and, curbing every spontaneous and fortuitous instinct, he desired that every detail should be pondered over at length. From his research into pure proportions to his figures of the most hybrid monsters, everything had to appear natural and rational.
(Johann Wolfgang Goethe, *Italian Journey*, 1816)

All that Giotto and Masaccio had attained in the rendering of tactile values, all that Fra Angelico or Filippo had achieved in expression, all that Pollaiuolo had accomplished in movement, or Verrocchio in light and shade, Leonardo, without the faintest trace of that tentativeness, that painfulness of effort which characterized his immediate precursors, equalled or surpassed... And if Leonardo has been left behind as a painter of light, no one has succeeded in conveying by means of light and shade a more penetrating feeling of mystery and awe than he in his *Virgin of the Rocks*. Add to all this a feeling for beauty and significance that have scarcely ever been approached... Leonardo is the one artist of whom it may be said with perfect literalness: Nothing that he touched but turned into a thing of eternal beauty. Whether it be the cross-section of a skull, the structure of a weed, of a study of muscles, he, with his feeling for line and for light and shade, for ever transmuted it into life-communicating values; and all without intention, for most of these magical sketches were dashed off to illustrate purely scientific matter, which alone absorbed his mind at the moment.
(B. Berenson, *The Italian Painters of the Renaissance*, London 1896)

Nor was Leonardo immune from the human weakness of despising what one does not know and does not possess. On numerous occasions his determined position as rigorous naturalist showed signs of becoming narrow-minded in a way which was typical of those who do not see any other activity as being worthwhile apart from their own. From this derived his advice not to meddle in "those things which the human mind is not capable of and which it is not possible to demonstrate by means of natural example." That which could not be given a mathematical basis, for him, was non-existent... What we must look for in Leonardo is certainly not a system, which is lacking, but the meaning and importance of a number of observations occurring in his writing that concern aspects of truth which are then explained and justified by the subsequent development of his line of thinking. Thus it is quite remarkable that Leonardo should have generally tended to consider art, especially painting, as a theoretical matter, or a form of knowledge, or "science" as he put it. "If you despise painting, which is the only imitator of all the manifest works of nature, it is certain that you will equally despise a subtle invention, which with philosophical and fine speculation considers all the classes of forms: seas, places, plants, animals, grasses and flowers, which are surrounded by light and shade. And truly this is science, and the legitimate child of nature, because painting is brought forth by nature." Painting never appeared to him merely as an instrument of pleasure, or a means of obtaining practical ends. His mathematical ideal of science, in the presence of his knowledge of painting, caused him some embarrassment. However, he recognised that painting offered something more than, or different from, what mathematics could offer. Geometry and arithmetic

"do not expatiate on anything except information regarding continuous or discontinuous quantities, but they are not concerned with quality, which is the beauty of the works of nature and the ornament of the world." His passion for experience and for the concrete caused him to insist on the value of certainty that art possesses, in that it is sure of the certainty which is so characteristic of the senses. "Painting deals with the appearances, colours and forms of anything created by nature. And philosophy penetrates the same bodies, observing in them its own virtue, but it is not satisfied by the truth produced by the painter, who keeps to himself the fundamental truth of such bodies, so that the eye might be less beguiled."
(B. Croce, "Leonardo filosofo," in *Leonardo*, 1939)

His aesthetic doctrine was unknown until the publication of the manuscripts. Only in 1651 was the *Treatise on Painting* printed, and this was based on a transcript of the sixteenth century. Leonardo's wide-ranging studies had led him to a complete cosmological concept which united heaven and earth in the pulsations of a universe brought alive by radiated light and driven by the constant struggle of the elements. In particular these included water, the basis of the blue atmosphere in which the backgrounds of his paintings were steeped. The crowning glory of all doctrinal wisdom was for him painting, which was the only medium which allowed the beauty and richness of

form to be completely extolled.
(A. Chastel, *Storia dell'arte italiana*, 1982)

However, it was Milan that gave birth to Leonardo the theoretician and man of science. His scientific vocation had its origins in his encounter with men of letters, a category which included philosophers, theologians, physicians and, in general, students of the so-called liberal arts. In contrast with them Leonardo represented the world of the "manual" or "menial" arts. It was a social hierarchy which dated back to ancient times, when free men avoided manual work in order to dedicate themselves to purely intellectual activities, in other words the humanities and philosophy with all the sciences and politics. Physical work in contact with the impure matter was reserved for slaves, freedmen and illiterates, rising up the social scale to artisans and artists, who were still considered, however, to be part of the category of the "manual arts." Leonardo could not abide the underestimation of his art. Painting had to be included with the liberal arts, in so far as it was a science due to its rich store of theory and because it did not confine itself to depicting the surfaces of objects, but it penetrated them and revealed their internal properties and the pulsation of vital energies.
(A. Marinoni, "Il Codice Atlantico," in *Leonardo all'Ambrosiana, il Codice Atlantico, i disegni di Leonardo e della sua cerchia*, edited by A. Marinoni and L. Cogliati Arano, 1982)

The very high opinion which Leonardo had of painting and, consequently, the leading role among all the other artists which he assigned to the painter, led him to speak about an analogy with divine power. But this did not happen because of the typically Renaissance exaltation of the human being as the key figure of the world, but rather through the consciousness of unequalled independent power given to the artist who stands before Nature... As a painter, Leonardo made every effort to attain his own personal style, which was the one that allowed him to surpass the ideals of drawing and plasticity of the Florentine tradition in order to obtain a fully pictorial effect. In this style he attained the fervour of life as it was happening, almost mysteriously, with the imperceptible vibration of shadow, light and tone. It was also the ideal which he had developed by the observation of the world which surrounded him, preferring to be out at twilight in order to enjoy greater intimacy with nature and a subtler, more penetrating exploration of the secrets of life.
(V. Mariani, "Le idee di Leonardo sulla pittura," in *Leonardo da Vinci*, 1984)

Leonardo was right. It was not possible to liken him to contemporary architects, forgers of cannon and so on. This was not because he so brilliantly outshone them all, but because he was concerned with totally different questions. They made weapons of war and built fortresses. He, on the other hand, produced

ideas, which were not mere conjectures, but the outcome of the interaction of brain, eye and hand. That is to say he forged himself. His temerity was too magnificent for it to be written off as mere arrogance. It was something else, at least from a historical point of view. It was, in fact, thanks to the chaotic and unfinished state of his projects that in many cases Leonardo's work obtained, with extraordinary completeness, an original result that had not been entirely foreseen. In the immense contradictory alternation of these projects—which was not referable to any common denominator existing among Leonardo's inventions and initiatives—and in their variety, the Inventor was devised, the Conceiver was planned and the singular model of cultural creativity as an end in itself was developed. This gives particular interest to the figure of Leonardo in this century, when, for the first time, culture has become so problematic regarding itself... Michelangelo was the greatest artist of the Renaissance because he was quite simply obliged to be nothing but an artist. Precisely for this reason, his task lay outside the field of art. It was no mere coincidence that Michelangelo's creations became increasingly "non-aesthetic," astonishingly intense, unbearable and non-classical—to put it another way non-Renaissance. For Michelangelo art was obtained by dint of hard physical work, with the carving of stone, with the enervating introjection in the matter, in order to create it again from within... Leo-nardo developed this idea of a universal "science of painting," that is to say an understanding which is both alienated and investigative of what there is in the world, right up to the furthermost limit which astounded his contemporaries. The whole of his creative thought involved an Intellect which observed from an alienated point of view, which looked with attention. He was, in other words, a painter who had reached such heights of folly that he could not possibly have been limited by painting or art in general and who was, indeed, obliged not to be an artist. Art was not bestowed upon him, it was perceived by insight. Leonardo was the greatest artistic project of the Renaissance.
(L.M. Batkin, *Leonardo da Vinci*, 1988)

Essential Bibliography
L'opera completa di Leonardo pittore, edited by A. Ottino della Chiesa, Milan 1967.

C. Pedretti, *Leonardo. A Study in Chronology and Style*, London 1973.

A.M. Brizio, "Leonardo pittore," in *Leonardo*, edited by L. Reti, Milan 1974.

Leonardo. La pittura, Florence 1977, 2nd ed. 1985.

Leonardo da Vinci, Disegni anatomici della Biblioteca Reale di Windsor, catalogue of the exhibition, Palazzo Vecchio, Florence 1979.

C. Pedretti, *Leonardo*, Bologna 1979.

M. Rosci, *Leonardo*, Milan 1979.

S.J. Freedberg, *The Pelican History of Art, Painting in Italy 1500-1600*, Harmondsworth, Middlesex, 1979.

Leonardo da Vinci—Nature Studies from the Royal Library at Windsor Castle, catalogue of the exhibition by Carlo Pedretti, introduction by Kenneth Clark, 1981, Royal Academy of Arts, London.

Leonardo da Vinci—The Codex Hammer formerly the Codex Leicester, catalogue of the exhibition by Jane Roberts, introduction by Carlo Pedretti, 1981, Royal Academy of Art, London.

Leonardo e l'età della ragione, edited by E. Bellone and P. Rossi, Milan 1982.

Leonardo e Milano, edited by G.A. Dell'Acqua, Milan 1982.

Frederick Hartt, *History of Italian Renaissance Art*, London 1987.

Leonardo scomparso e ritrovato, catalogue of the exhibition, Palazzo Medici Riccardi, Florence 1988.

L.M. Batkin, *Leonardo da Vinci*, Bari 1988.

Leonardo da Vinci, catalogue of the exhibition, Hayward Gallery, London 1989.

P.C. Marani, *Leonardo e i leonardeschi nei musei della Lombardia*, Milan 1990.